A Subversive Mind
A Vision

A Subversive Mind

❖

A Vision

Maysaa Haydar

Claddagh Ltd.
Florida

A Subversive Mind
A Vision

Claddagh Ltd. Publishing House

For information address:
Claddagh Ltd.
www.CladdaghPublishing.com

ISBN: 978-0-9795213-2-4

Printed in the United States of America

In dedication to you...

Contents

Prologue

Section Three

Prologue

It really doesn't matter who have written this book…
It can be regarded as a series of discoveries rather
than an invention by itself. Any person is accessing
what will be propounded; this book can help her or
him become conscious or more conscious of the
subject-matter.

This book is meant to be a peaceful manifesto and not
a harangue or libel against any person, dogma, or
system despite its decisive and poignant stances and
views.

I am a Middle Eastern woman. I have evolved greatly
and extensively in terms of modes of thought and
believe that I still am.

I mean that you find my book enjoyable and meaningful so good luck...

Note:
The unconventional use of language is intentional, for instance when I talk of God I don't use the generic-he, instead I use she and he because it would be a more faithful reference to all facets of creation: creation contains the feminine as well as the masculine.

It's all about patterns of thought and stances of relativity. The generic-he conveys a political message which I don't support. Its religious message is that the masculine created the feminine or that the feminine came to existence only because the masculine- created beforehand- was in need for the feminine, conveying that the masculine is the superior and the more elementary and potent entity as religion upholds, reminiscent of Adam's ennui in heaven before Eve.

Creation is a simultaneous phenomenon and a delicate balance and unity. There's a mutual need and subtle balance and viable interdependence between both aspects. I am neither a sexist nor a female-chauvinist. I just seek the Truth which I don't purport to possess but meagerly.

Furthermore, the views and ideas depicted here are inspired by prior discoveries and scientific and spiritual pursuits. Any acknowledgement is automatically, faithfully, and gratefully paid.

Section One

The Human Heritage

People have evolved from animals. Their physique allows them a certain spiritual capacity. Some believe that the awaited resurrection day will be affiliated with a DNA-upgrade to our species which will increase our spiritual capacity, making us more spiritual beings. This is reminiscent of religion's vague stress on the importance of believing in resurrection day.

Each form of life embodies a certain spirituality which manifests itself in all facets of its existence from what kind of sustenance it subsists on to its behavior, intelligence, mating habits, waste products, material body architecture...

Nothing can overwhelm the power of fate: God's plan. I think that she and he have intended to endow us with our jarring potentials of good and evil, to contribute via the essences of energy we embody and propagate to the spiritual evolution of the universe. Knowing and unraveling one's fate is not a passive experience but rather involved. One's fate is the potential of one's Self, to reconcile our ego to our fate, which may sound so inclemently hostile, foreign, and detached, is to love one's Self: the greatest value in life.

Human potential is all-inclusive of our spiritual capacity, of our palpable history, our variable knowledge and embodiment of wisdom andtruth, and even of the minutia of our experiences, pretty much everything inherent or accessible to us to know or to do, since when we access a certain potential of knowledge and experience we access it in ourselves. One can't know or perceive what is beyond her or his Self by virtue of our limited potential and relative consciousness (relative karma and relative capacity), whether it be relatively good and joyous or horrific and distressing.

All aspects of creation are meant to propagate goodness, what some refer to as "the expansion of happiness". Individual discrete instances may attest otherwise, with them being the disembodiment of wisdom and balance seemingly. What is on the surface level labeled bad is the good of another subtler level. There's no happening in the whole universe with no wisdom inherent to it since all experience and all happenings are but a potential in the mind of God, with an inscrutable subtle balance and divine reason governing them. But then, our relative awareness of these happenings is strictly relevant to our relative awareness of time and to our limited wisdom and thought potential. If we were aware of time in a more transcendental way, we will be able to fathom the value of a happening in a different way, after fathoming all its other inherent potentials and values, the balance it engenders to the universe as a whole, and the essences it propagates and propounds or exhausts. Alas, we fall short and get overwhelmed. Our relative awareness of time makes us emphasize the manifest and the material, which produces a spiritual and emotional void. It's like we can't experience all dimensions of time so we get overwhelmed by its discrete happenings, our personal experiences, the history we are living, perceiving their impressions emphatically.

Our potential for happiness is variable and ambivalent. We are variably and momentarily stripped of our semblance of happiness. I say semblance because if we were purely happy, then our happiness wouldn't have contained any potential to fall from grace and lapse into sadness. Both states of mind exist relatively in symbiosis, with each containing the potential for the other.

All happenings contribute to good, even rape, war, and many hideous and evil other instances. They vent up stressful, latent complexes of spiritual ignorance that without their expression materially, the only way to make us conscious of them, life won't progress. They increase our awareness of what is quiescent and innate in us. Self-evidently, increased awareness is the first step to the increase of health, spiritual knowledge, and happiness. We experience a lot of pain, anguish, illness, and other unhappy states of mind and being. Bad experiences are knowledge of what we can be, our potential and karma, often what we deny as being a part of our Selves and can't cope with and transcend. Bad experiences extirpate our awareness of our fragile happiness: we won't be aware of happiness anymore instead stress will domineer and steer our consciousness. Our classical reactions to stress tend to create more stress.

We lack wisdom. All experience we witness is the experience we become more aware of, from the bubbling underhand potentials of our spirit. Wisdom is distinct at times from intelligence which may exploit the power of consciousness for gross reasons, intentions, and experiences, the thing which backdrops our intellectual capacity.

Universal as well as human phenomena would be much more facile to explain if perused in terms of essences of energy. That's why there is a concept of karma, it engendering a balance or answer or consummation to some experience initiated before. You have propagated or embodied an essence and you are getting the essence back with a change to the dimensions and relativity of the experience. It's like making advances to the tree of knowledge, you initiate a certain experience and life wants you to get as fully aware of the nature, meaning, and impact of your action as possible within the capacity of human consciousness. There are different levels of action: thought, intent, desire, mood, physical activity...

Some crimes are paid before they are committed, they say. It's karma which has shuffled the sequence but not changed the essences. The crime was ineluctable.

We are self-conscious of our superior intelligence to animate and to what we vainly term "inanimate" creation. Our relatively superior intelligence is tacitly due to our evolved nervous system. Intelligence, when it contributes to harm, always castrates itself, by the reverberation of its actions and intent, and by it not embodying wisdom on a subjective level. On the objective level, our intelligence embodies wisdom by the virtue of knowing the laws of nature and employing them creatively, and relentlessly. On the subjective level and because our technology has been employed injuriously, we have not embodied the goodness of knowledge, and thus have castrated our Selves and hindered our progression on all levels, with always in the background the threat of an imminentand terrible retribution.

History has depicted humans as ignorant, authorative, greedy, material, sexist, brutal, bestial... There have been wars and all the infamous and heinous exploits done in its frenzy: epic rapes and enslavement, mass torture and mutilation, brutal and unfeeling killing... There has been sheer wickedness in politics, too numberous and versatile to becall. There has been sexism, ironically with women contributing much to its perpetuation. There has been a crooked sexuality, bestial, promiscuous, loveless, and imbalanced. We have lived an existence desiccated of wisdom and consequently of bliss and beauty. We have been living a gross materialism with lack of "spiritual morality", as distinct from "social morality".

God has created man as a chain in the series of the evolution of species. God has endowed humanity with certain potentials. Our history is part of our potential. It has been infamous. Our evils were necessary to the subtle balance of energies in this universe. We have latent in us both potentials for good and evil. I believe in fate. We were ordained to make such a history. The unraveling of fate is an "involved" experience and not something foreign or unindigenous imposed on us. Despite my contempt and repulsion, I have accepted our history as part of us and of our potential. We can't do or experience, with action a form of knowledge, what is not inherent in us, not our potential.

Relation of Consciousness to Experience

Imagine it's your wedding day after a while. You are experiencing beforehand its backward reverberations. You are frenzifully entrenched in its ambiance and preparations. You have always tried to envision your wedding day. You are attempting to reach and emulate your consciousness of the actual experience, with all its infinite versatilities and details, as if it's happening and you are there. By comparison of both consciousness, the dreamy and yearning one with that of the actual experience, your imaginative experience fails and falls short.

Why? Our imagination is a form of intelligence and consciousness, and because of our limited thought potential and wisdom, our imagination is not efficient and real. We can't create the experience we imagine. We can't imagine what we experience. However, we experience psychologically what we imagine. It's a level of experience, inefficient to create reality and dubious as whether to be harmless or harmful to a person's well-being.

Our reality is a potential in the mind of god. Our lives and our potential is an experience in God's imagination. We are more airy than we think.

What we experience engenders a consciousness and emanates from a potential. Reality proximates wisdom because it's more immediately governed by the laws of God than what we imagine or envision. It's like ingesting processed or non-processed foods. Our imagination is relatively more processed than our actuality. That's why Plato called an artist "thrice an imitator". The artist's imagination envisages shadows of what is real.

If we are emanations from God's consciousness, then how come we err and that what we imagine and propound can be of an unwise nature?

All material experiences, whether they be internal or external, communicate, illuminate, or unravel a certain spiritual purpose, essence, and capacity, the externalization of which is the cornerstone for the spiritual progression of the material: spiritual progression being the ultimate purpose of the material movement which fuels the evolution of material manifestations.

The best one can do with a material experience is to make peace with it and forget it, since to progress spiritually and materially is to liberate oneself and one's potential and awareness from the past and the material experiences relative and related to it: what is left pending of the embodiment of spiritual knowledge. To emphasize a material experience is stressful, a displaced and castrated act of awareness since all material manifestations are but shadows of the spiritual essence and purpose. This emphasis will elicit material as well as emotional bondage since the energies of one's state of consciousness are being channeled in the direction of the treacherous material manifestations. If one focuses on the relative specifics (form and vehicle: perception, conception, physical situation), one will miss the spiritual value it serves, and will get overwhelmed by the stress engendered by it being an act of spiritual ignorance. Thus, emotional bondage attaches and aggregates exorbitantly excessive emotion and awareness on material aspects or experiences that are but transient, limited, and relative.

We are more emotionally bound to the object, person, or situation towards which we owe negative attitudes and emotions rather than that we love. It's a cliché but since love is a higher spiritual quality, an embodiment of wisdom and happiness, love actually sets our consciousness free, engendering serenity and wellbeing. In accordance, if an experience is perceived as negative, thus focusing on its material and superficial aspects, hard feelings and negative attitudes will invade our being. The question is: if a situation is truly negative, does owing to it negative emotions and attitudes will help resolve it wholesomely and progressively? If a situation is negative, will it be of any use to contribute and confer more negativity?

To rationalize about the experiences we've witnessed and perceived is one of the most meaningful activities to our entities. Is not that directing potential to one's material existence? Ironically, yes, our experiences naturally incite us to react to them by unraveling the potential of our Selves, the crucial variable in our reaction is how much we're embodying and seeking the higher spiritual values like the spirit of love, peace, forgiveness, and balance. The discrepancy between spiritual contemplation and material and emotional bondage lies in the difference of emphasis and prospects since contemplation has its conscious goals and intent the moral and spiritual progress of the human Self in terms of the increased knowledge and embodiment of the higher spiritual values. All in all, contemplation regards material experience as a spiritual revelation.

Sufficely, if some material experience of the past still holds one's entity in emotional bondage, thus, the foregone past persists to be a psychological reality- still forceful, effective, and inexorable, progression on all levels will not be efficient.

We are created with both potentials to know and embody wisdom, or to negate wisdom and bliss, but because all creation serves a good purpose, the role of karma here emerges as a balance and the bitter way to wisdom and synergy in life.

The Spiritual Evolution of the Universe

Evolution of life forms is based on a oneness: a continuity and a unity. Every material phenomenon is relative to a specific time and to a specific spiritual signification. On the level of the Absolute, all these three variables, with their endless versatility, are one.

Destruction is the most materially powerful force, radical, relentless, and harsh, with utmost brevity and efficacy. The destruction of material aspects is a perpetual phenomenon in life and the universe, and simultaneous with the transformation of energies on a subtle level, the latter manifesting itself in the birth of new forms of life.

How nostalgically does science becall ancient eras of life on earth, extinct species, and the ever-present moment of chaotic creation! The Big Bang is the archetype destroyer, of the vacuum of space what is now known as Black Energy.

All the universe and life thrive on the aspect of destruction for the purpose of evolution, the latter being the unraveling of subtle potentials. Energies are processed and transformed whether in the animate or prejudicially inanimate, as well as in the manifest and unmanifest, realms. The universe is dynamic; it's still expanding charged with the massive impetus of the Big Bang. Hints of its imminent destruction are extant: Black holes, which are ironically also a mechanism to restore a momentary balance to the impetus of expansion. They are a phenomenon of gravity, a counterbalance to expansion. Otherwise, the concept of synergy and unity of the universe would be expired.

On subatomic and atomic levels, all forms of life are made of the self-same particles and energies, of the self-same undifferentiated essence. Each form of life is an emanation from an equation in the mind of God, from a potential. On this subtle level, all forms of life, matter (inorganic and organic), wind, fire, light, and other creations are one: the omni-presence of God.

Evolution of life has started from elementary forms. A theory is that elementary energies have transformed themselves into subatomic particles and then these formed the nucleus and electrons of undifferentiated atoms. These undifferentiated atoms then metamorphosed themselves into differentiated forms: the molecules of minerals. Minerals comprise the source and the backbone of some of the inorganic matter as well as all of the organic matter. In any case, light energy is the source from which all life emanates; it's the dual creation of Black Energy.

All material phenomena are entwined with relative and specific spiritual significations and purpose. Every material or physical experience, manifestation, or event is always relevant to a specific time and circumstance, and is but one of an infinite potential. We use such terms as "infinity, eternity, and boundless" to mark limits and spiritual capacities only comprehended by God, omnipotent and omnipresent in all time and creation, and also transcendental to them.

On a material level, evolution of life forms has been spurred by certain galactic or natural events, by the need created by a universe that expands and metamorphoses its life forms and experience endlessly, to externalize all of its spiritual potentials till exhaustion of its limitless limit, the day that the universe ends and disintegrates, destroying itself into a hypothetical re-birth. As the universe tends to expand, its life forms expand also, certain potentials unravel each at its time. On a tangible level, causes of evolution may range anywhere from cosmic and galactic events and explosions, ecological changes, to other extreme natural phenomenon. It's convenient to envision evolution as a need of life to adapt and survive or as an exigent transformation into another level of existence spurred by radical stimuli, as in bacteria evolving into the elementary forms of species, or as in humans evolving into a new species with a radically higher spiritual capacity, as a future possibility, when our species' spirituality will get evolved till its exhaustion.

Something has churned inorganic matter in its five elements (water, air, fire, space, earth) to metamorphose into the most elementary form of organic life: an undifferentiated form of bacteria, which in turn metamorphosed itself into the most elementary and undifferentiated form of plant life. In turn, the latter metamorphosed itself into more evolved and variable species of plants over the passage of time and in response to various natural and life events. Similarly, a form of undifferentiated bacteria evolved itself later into the most elementary form of animal life, which then differentiated and evolved itself into variable species of animals. The same applies to other life categories (fungi, virus…).

Furthermore, evolution of life forms on earth commenced from sea-life then to amphibious forms and lastly to land creatures. Evolution is an ever on-going process.

All creation is a conduit and the vehicle of a spiritual formula in the mind of God. The whole of creation is a manifestation of a potential of the soul. Inanimate creations are not without spirituality. Even the chaos and destruction anterior to creation are not without spiritual significations and quiddities. The material evolution of the universe gives us an infinity of life forms, each emanating from a soul or a natural law transcendental formula, and each according to its form, physique, and nature has a certain relative potential of spiritual capacity and evolution, and a certain spiritual purpose in the Grand Architecture of the universe. These "souls" or spiritual formulas can be perused as subtle energies in synergy and in union with each other, the essences of versatile, endless, and ever-changing life forms and material natures, essences that have an indigenous predilection for metamorphoses.

All the universe evolves spiritually. What we label inanimate as planets, galaxies, and so on, evolve spiritually as well as us, but of course each on its relatively discrete level of existence.

Presuming wrongfully and egotistically, human beings are the sole animate creatures that evolve spiritually, via a communion or recourse to an omnipresent and transcendental entity we call God. Thus, we can say that the whole life on earth has evolved materially and physically to give us a creature of a certain spiritual capacity called a human, reconciling both scientific and religious views. This is only partially true... I believe it's tacit that human beings can't be the most spiritual or immediate to God of all creation.

The Formula of Fate

If God knows and has created everything, then there is something called fate. If we are God's created creatures, and we acknowledge that we have limitations in terms of consciousness, physique, and experience (material and spiritual), then we are somehow pre-conditioned creatures by the innate nature of our entity. We have a limited and relative potential, and God knows exactly our potential and our evolution through time, so we are first and foremost expectable relatively to God or to some creature with a higher spirituality.

Probability in Maths studies how much a certain event has chances to occur among a multitude of other events. So, we can say that among a plethora, each potential event has a certain chance or ratio of occurring, and this is only relative to one experience. We can say that God copes with the absolute potentials, of all times and life, of boundless numbers and experiences we can't even imagine.

But then, why in fact a certain thing happens and not another of a plethora of potentials in a certain probability? Find the formula mathematicians of what explains why the conditions of life elicit or propound a certain event to happen exclusively among a multitude of potentials, an inscrutable life formula of relativity between what actually happens and what are the numberous potentials. Add to it a dimension of eternity, of the infinite potentials of life, of the way they occur in mutual and viable conditioning, synergy and relativity, then you'll have the inscrutable formula of fate.

This is of course a joke and false solicitation. Our consciousness is relative and not absolute. Egocentric intellectual assumptions are always erroneous here and elsewhere. Egocentricity disrupts self-knowledge, wisdom, and happiness in accepting one's level of existence.

Reincarnation, Ghost, or Nihilism of the Human Soul

Does a human soul reincarnate or transform into a ghost upon death? Or does it disappear into nihilism? Or does it metamorphose again after another physical death and gets its potential and karma rechanneled and manifest again in a new relativity of consciousness and experience, in a new transient life span?

If all creation in its endless versatile life forms is the manifestation of an Absolute spiritual potential, and all material phenomena are preconditioned by necessary spiritual significations and essences, these in turn being conditioned by God's plan or fate (the inherent architecture and subtle balance of the whole universe, life, and existence), we can apply the same principle to the human soul. The human soul is the relative absolute to a plethora of humans. Each human-physical phenomenon with specific spiritual capacities and significations- can be regarded as a manifest, material emanation-of a multitude- from the soul, with each emanation strictly relative to a specific time. We contribute to God's plan of the whole existence through our souls which denominate our relative existence, spiritual capacity, and consciousness with that of specific others of different times. Each is a cog in the process of the human soul unraveling its spiritual potentials (which elicit material phenomena), by the consciousness realizing itself through karma or yoga (intense or transcendental spiritual contemplation).

Furthermore, reincarnation is a prerequisite stipulation to the concept of karma. Karma is usually equated with bad karma, the bitter way to wisdom. Karma is a human's fate, of predetermined experiences and spiritual capacities, the inherent, viable, and crucial composite of the human soul. It's the law of action and reaction.

If karma is the bittersweet way to wisdom and self-knowledge and self-realization, yoga is the ideal surrogate. Yoga is an unperturbed direct communion to the Soul, the most immediate way to enlightenment. Some yoga are a technique to reduce stress so as to pave the way for spiritual revelation more immediately. Others are a purgatorial contemplation of life.

In case of enlightenment, the body (the physical, relative, discrete facet of existence) and the soul become one; the body won't be anymore a transient, restless vehicle of a plethora. The impurities will be purged and the person becomes the embodiment of wisdom and the spirit love, with no negativity whatsoever. The person will then transcend and metamorphose into another realm of existence. However, the enlighted person is not to be confused with God, since enlighted beings still belong to the manifest creation that can be somehow perceived and conceived by the mind. Furthermore, if a person practices yoga, it is not to be perused in isolation with other facets of his or her existence: it doesn't mean he or she is enlighted.

The religious philosophies concerning the transformation of a human's spirit into a ghost upon death, with its affairs pending till Judgment Day, is a blurry dictum. "Why blurry?", because it doesn't explain what are the spiritual undertones or reasons of the world's movement, the outcome of which it clearly prophesizes apocalyptically. It doesn't explain spiritually how fate acts. It oversimplifies karma in terms of God's trials.

To religion, the ghost has in its resume both evil and good, so it's self-evidently not to be equated with the Soul which is utterly pure. Here is the contradiction and short-coming. Religion slymns that the human spirit transforms into a ghost. What happens to the soul? It goes back to God... Has it ever been not immediate to God? Or is the human spirit (relative consciousness) equated with the soul (transcendent level of creation) and the soul is transformed into a ghost? If this is true, then no communion- which is a continual process of spiritual revelation- with God and thus spiritual evolution would have been possible. All would have been a sheer material existence underlayed with stagnation, monotony, and vapidity. Then, the human soul would be the ego, and a human ego is nothing but a transient phase and phenomenon in the process of the expansion consciousness. Consequently, this is an egocentric explanation of a spiritual matter, investing God and the Soul with traits of our relative and limited consciousness.

On the other hand, nihilistic attitudes in general fail to provide happiness and emotional well-being, being sheerly material. Nihilistic concepts are tacitly extirpated since it has been depicted that the whole creation is based on a viable interdependence and subtle balance of all life forms, times, energies, and material phenomena and spiritual significations.

There is no consensus about one theory concerning reincarnation. Some religions even have inoculated a material, sexist, or bigot spirit into their philosophies of reincarnation.

Section Two

The World System: The Disillusionment

The World System or the Establishment is supposedly
humanity's sensational and potent achievement, the
crystallization of a certain fate and spiritual capacity.
It insinuates and comprises various social institutions,
dogmas, patterns of thought, and innate predilections
of humans. Relative and specific modes and ethos of
religion, army, social mores, money, sexuality, and
politics have externalized out of relative and specific
spiritual capacity and indigenous tendencies. Thus,
it's all an expression of the collective human
consciousness, karma, and the spiritual purpose of a
preordained fate and potential.

The human heritage and history are the manifest
effects of this World System upon life and this world.
I have already adumbrated at our heinous exploits
but not attempted to explain the social reasons,
enterprises, and mechanisms which have propounded
and inoculated such an infamous history, ignorance,
and evil.

My stipulation is that human culture and civilization
are basically unspiritual, civilized only in a primitive,
barbaric, and material sense.

Society

Freud has defined a human as a social, political animal, which has been a valid banner to the history and collective consciousness of humans, antithetical and dissonant to another questionable definition: a human is a spiritual being, since history and the current moment attest otherwise, since even the relatively spiritual are helpless and spirituality is still an unreached and frail ideal.

Human society is at the center of the Establishment. It can be perused as the source and the field of action of all the issues pertaining to humans. Religion, politics, and other facets of the Establishment all emanate from the social ethos and the collective level of consciousness.

Many intellectuals attribute corruption as a basic trait of human society. So, where does corruption start? Is money and a human's material nature the source of corruption? Or is it the prevailing promiscuous and imbalanced sexuality? Is it politics? Is it the religious institution? Is it indifference? One cannot fail but to see that corruption and the lack of wisdom and the spirit of love permeate all facets of our existence. Corruption can't be isolated and conferred to a certain area of our lives, since life is a continuity and all aspects of human life exist in symbiosis and are on a subtle level but one. Everything in life is contagious and affects most immediately the forms of life on its level of existence.

I believe that corruption starts manifesting in the basic human mores and bonds that govern and limit the relationship of one human to another with a material, suspicious, exploitative, and wary spirit. It starts in the way one human considers another. It starts in the hierarchy of authority, unequal distribution of wealth, prejudice, injustice, exploitation, and ignorance, pretty much everything that expresses lack of the higher spiritual values. Humans have always purported to vie for justice and equality, that's why the mouth-piece of Democracy Aristotle has perused women as inferior beings and slaves as no beings at all. This proves that our conception of higher values is limited and relative to time and to our relative spiritual capacity entwined to it.

Social morality is distinct from spiritual morality, and historically has sanctioned outrageous things such as war, slavery, and various other injustices and bestialities. Christ has pronounced this demarcation and this criticism. Social morality is not spiritual since it elicits and embodies a spirit of materialism and spiritual shallowness. Social mores propound basic political messages, they are the elementary dogma and patterns of thought which when processed will become a certain kind of politics. Throughout history, these social mores are self-evidently been based on patriarchy, sexism, and despotism.

Is not social judgment based on appearances and an iniquitous variable of power, with either a spirit of unconscious fawning or of self-righteous victimizing? Are not people egocentric and proud? With a world and history like ours, can we even pretend to be close to God and to have embodied the dictums and spirit of God in our ways, from the corny minutia to our hefty actions, choices, and values?

Social morality translates a certain relativity of
consciousness. Knowledge from India demarcates
that our world has been flopping in the first three
primitive charkas (fight for survival, sexual
gratification and procreativity, and authority). Society
has made laws and institutions of law, the thing that
expresses that the spirit of insecurity, suspicion,
treachery, and transgression are extremely potent
elements. The global census, and a gross sexuality
desiccated of its spiritual and physical balance is
another fact. The charka of authority manifests in the
social hierarchy of patriarchy, sexism, and the epic
exploitation of the masses taking the multifarious
faces of despotism from slavery, serfdom, sweat-shop,
monarchy, aristocracy, bourgeoisie, to globalization.
A minority reaches the summit of riches and social
authority on the back, blood, and tears of subservient
and oblivious others (I don't mean those who have
earned their wealth decently and honestly and even
have been generous and humanitarian with it). This
is another formula of the mutual interplay of
ignorance.

Have there been any general spirit and collective
attitude embodying compassion and love, instead of
grossness and exploitation? Have not we been
prejudiced and material? Have we not lied and

sinned? Have we not forgotten God and obliterated his and her presence from our consciousness while we perpetrate our evils? Have we not socially justified our sins as some leverage or some act of heroism and identity instead of due to some ignorance? Have we beseeched forgiveness and amendment, or we don't need to because we feel secure within the customs or within the unacknowledged dirty facts? Do we really appreciate the truth? Are we more prone to victimize and exploit than to help and forgive?

Questions like these can never end.

Laws are made to organize the affairs of humans and rather to protect them from each other. The social institution have thus confessed its foregone failure in making people good, the thing that justifies its fear and need to issue laws. If our lives and psyches were ideal, then there would be no potential for evil, and then there would be no need for laws and their reinforcement. Alas, people err and transgress and can't rely on their relative consciousness to embody goodness and wisdom.

There are such things as crimes and criminals, even seen as heroes at times. Criminals are the best tangible evidence of the failure of society to make of them "good citizens". In fact, criminals may be perused as a naked, blunt, and injurious truth, emanating from our collective spirituality which has sprouted and elicited such perversions, due to our collective lack of wisdom. They resemble and relate to the relatively good in crucial ways. We are the same humanity.

Patriarchy has been the prevailing system of human affairs. It is based on sexism and vital obsessions with property and political power.

Patriarchy has claimed to have replaced and corrected the chaos and corruption of pre-patriarchal times, namely, of communal life. Of course, it is a plain and naked contradiction to what patriarchy is actually. The corruption, namely the communal sexuality, has been replaced by the corruption of the harem, which are nothing but the property of potent and powerful men. Sexual promiscuity and bestiality still are rampant as the dominant attitude and penchant of humans. Why? Clearly, Patriarchy is inherently castrated from spirituality and wisdom, for political power and property comprise its essence and ultimate purpose. It can be perused as a set of intellectual egocentric assumptions: our intellect always falls short of spiritual truth.

* A Vision *

The innate sexism of patriarchy is embodied by both men and women. This ignorance does not put in confrontation men and women as persons, instead the balance and knowledge of feminine and masculine values and principles are undermined.

Women being the breeders of peoples, inoculating and molding their spirits so that the latter's potentials of thought and spirituality, dogma, and attitude would bear the vital insignia and effect of the first. Women have been upholding the sexist spirit which mutilates and consolidates their entities. They have been victimized, exploited, and persecuted first and foremost by their own device. Otherwise, this iniquity wouldn't have underscored a long history. The systemized and internalized persecution of women is historically intertwined with the systemized and internalized persecution of peoples. Anton Saade has said, "The face of my mother is the face of my nation."

Sexism directly sanctions iniquity and injustice towards women through the social mores and pervading prejudices. Women are treated and judged by double-standards and are often victimized with various degrees of harshness by other women and men. A woman is the entity most liable of dehumanization and public condemnation. Furthermore, the fair sex has been economically

emasculated via deprivation of education and
property. Inheritance of wealth has always
marginalized women as well as social double-
standards. Women have prostrated themselves, in
willing humiliation to their entities, internalizing and
propounding the political dogmas of patriarchy that
are inherently brutal and unjust.

Sexism is a potent element extant in the ethos of
patriarchy and is manifest in countless life
circumstances and aspects. In a brutal, inclement
political world, women are the most politically
undermined entity. All in all, patriarchy isn't and
can't be the salvation and the ideal deliverance of
human society.

Thus, society is a political organization, with a
hierarchy of authority, and collective mores and
attitudes serving a political purpose. Self-evidently,
spiritual concerns are out of the picture since wisdom
jars headlong with the inherent political essence of the
social system. Nevertheless, this political essence has
been evolving, at least on a superficial level.

Religion

Religion might be regarded as the greatest political hoax of all time, especially if gauged to be an ironical mixture of social patriarchal values and some of the most beautiful and eternal wisdom. The religious institution has purported to be the salvation of humanity. Has there been any real salvation?

When we talk about religion it's better to talk about the religious institution. After all, religion hopefully is not just about spirituality and wisdom, it's a full-fledged, full-blown institution. It's a multifaceted enterprise of politics and economics.

Religion contributes to politics indirectly by socially and mentally conditioning humans via perpetuating the dogma, hierarchy, attitudes, and values, namely of patriarchy. Religion also underpins these with ecclesiastic justifications, rationalizations, and sagas so as to invest them with an inscrutable and ineffable sense- displaced, transcendental qualities of God. Religious dogma relies mainly on intellectual egocentric presumptions reinforced by the fact that they are contextualized in the ambiance of myth. Cultural myths inspire awe (in contrast to wonder inspired by spiritual revelations), which is an epic emotion. Awe then impresses the political messages on the intellect. Thus, we keep on projecting on religious dogma, rituals, and figures an aura of transcendentalism and spirituality. We rely on them for what we think is our spiritual health whereas in fact they are mechanical, stagnant, remote (projection is on an object outside the Self), and vapid. It's now a cliché that the quest for wisdom and higher spirituality is an intimate and individual activity.

Self-knowledge and self-realization are introspective activities with windfall inspirations of wisdom, since a person is inspired and gifted with wisdom and can't create it with his or her intelligence the knowledge that belongs to the all-knowing Mind (the Mind of 100% intelligence). On the other hand, the religious institution is renowned for direct political intervention and dominion. So, religion mainly

thrives on propounding dogma and rituals for a
political purpose.

Religion has been an abortive attempt at wisdom and
spirituality within the bounds of patriarchy. It's not a
coincidence that prophets were great icons of society:
kings, army leaders, wealthy tradesmen... Religion
has preached equality and justice "between men" and
other spiritual abstract values, but when it came to
the actual translation, religion actually has reinforced
a hierarchy of authority. On the other hand, the fact
that religion has reinforced sexist views and
chauvinism is a grand violation against God's created
feminine entities and principles. Furthermore, the
wars and their affiliating sadism perpetrated on the
behalf of religions pose as another major, dubious
issue. Hence, in a multitude of instances, religion has
actually elicited the most hideous evils.

Prophets have in overwhelming instances been
polygamous and even had harems. Polygamy and
harems are socially sanctioned formulas of sexuality,
an authorative leverage to men rising exponentially
with wealth, and both are imbalanced on both
physical and spiritual levels. Are not both a form of
debauchery and promiscuity?

It doesn't matter. They have been socially sanctioned.

Christ has preached monogamy which is still a far-reached ideal. Though I deal with the historical records and heritage with utmost skepticism, Christ has been the sole bearer of wisdom with no political and economic power affiliated to him.

All in all, when we bestow on the religion institution a certain social, political structure, dogma, and eventually power, with vital enormous "profits" and systemized economy, religion won't be anymore a matter of higher spiritual values nor about the ways of God. However, any person on a spiritual quest can find help and aid in everything, even in religion.

Religious rituals are social activities which reinforce and drum home attitudes and dogma. They create unconscious bondage inducing an underhand commiseration to a human's sense of lonesomeness and guilt. A basic joy of rituals is a tacit knowledge and emotional security that there are other fellow human beings who share one's world of mentality, quest for knowledge or power, and political stance. Religious rituals being social events are mechanical activities since one's quest for spirituality is by necessity a solitary or at least an introspective activity.

* A Vision *

All in all, the religious institution has been a vicarious recourse to people disconsolate about their lives and their world, insufferable of themselves, and thirsty for spirituality in a non-spiritually oriented world.

Sexuality

Sex is the most unresolved and uncontrolled of human issues. It's the scope where the intellect can't feign, trick, or cloak itself anymore and runs naked to its indigenous impulses, the impulses relative to a certain spirituality. Sex somehow levels all humans, from the highest intellectual to the most miserable illiterate. In a sexual act, the consciousness diffuses itself in its dimensions and spiritual significations.

Sexuality is the second most elementary part of the Self. In the context of a political and non-spiritually oriented world, sexuality manifests also the pervading ambiance. In many instances, sex has been divested of its spirituality and reduced into a mechanical, ritualistic, or bestial act.

Is sex conducive to spirituality? If so, why saints (enlighted men andwomen) have transcended it? Is abstinence good? Is license better and more matter-of-fact? Can't a sexual act be physically and emotionally balanced and wholesome enough to be a conduit for the embodiment of a higher spirituality?

Sex is conducive to a higher spirituality, only as said above as an emotionally and physically balanced act, when one unifies love and sex in one formula, one person, and one relationship. Love enlightens sex-love is wise, and wisdom seeks in everything what's healthy and meaningful to our spirits as well as to our bodies. Sex is not supposed to be a mere loveless, mechanical act to fill our emotional void or vent up licentiously our emotional disappointment since it's-indigenously- emotionally meaningful, inducing andembodying variously states of mind and being even though human society and the human intellect has corrupted, contorted, or misportrayed its essence. On the other hand, the emotional poignancy, intensity, and significance of sex can actually give impetus, vitality, and viability to one's spiritual quest.

Our sexuality is still very far from the ideal. So what is the ideal and what are the extant imbalances?

The ideal of sex is a life-long monogamy; a more up-to-date version is serial monogamy. Monogamy unifies a human's emotional and physical needs of self-fulfillment and satiation. It's the ideal formula that coalesces love and sex for the sake of emotional security and eventually a higher spirituality. Through monogamy, a human's sexual and spiritual drives reconcile and become one. Otherwise, a human being would bear an irresolvable breach and contradiction between the different components of his or her entity. This would pose as a hindrance and quandary to one's spiritual progression, self-knowledge, and wellbeing.

If monogamy is the unifying principle of a human's spiritual and sexual drives, then the imbalances of sexuality are proliferate from polygamy, casual sex, sodomy, homosexuality, orgies, loveless sex, to promiscuity. What denominates them is that they are self-evidently not conducive to spirituality, in stead to emotional void and bondage, and materialism. These all objectify sex and dehumanize the relationship as well as the sexual partner, and ironically egotistically eroticize the sex.

For instance, polygamy and promiscuity objectify and down-trod human feelings of love, jealousy, and communion, ineluctably then these myriad relationships are dehumanizing. These may be perused as a physical indulgence not in tune with the oneness of the human entity and soul. Another instance is the extremely controversial homosexuality. Homosexuality is a highly eroticized trend, syndrome of an anterior imbalance, initiated among the relatively "straight relationships". Homosexual males are renowned for sodomy, but isn't sodomy in fact perpetrated on a wide scale in heterosexual relationships and marketed deviously and indelibly through porn? Homosexuality has many reasons that inoculate it anywhere from a broken home, bigotry, to a harsh father… Basically, it is an imbalanced attitude towards gender whether one's gender or the opposite sex, ensued by eroticized desires, of a person unwilling to wallow in a communion with the opposite sex so as to achieve a sense of self-fulfillment and wholeness, since wholeness is a product of communion between God's dually and equally created entities of feminity and masculinity. A teenager may hate his father and the concept of manhood as perceived by him to be brutal and embrace feminity. On the other hand, a woman may have a violent repulsion towards men and manhood and recourse to homosexuality…

All in all, homosexuality can be deemed to be the outcome and syndrome of the imbalanced mating habits originating in heterosexual relationships anywhere in the animal kingdom, and to be a matter of a repulsive attitude engendered by social issues relating to gender, like sexism, patriarchy, and the pattern and quiddity of personal and family relationships. The balance between female and male entities and principles in sexuality and in elsewhere seems to be seriously upset. The social and psychological imbalance (sexism) between feminine and masculine values propagates and procreates other imbalances in different aspects of our life.

To add, the sexual instinct is blunt in the sense that it is not as half as harmful as when the intellect and human consciousness exploit their creative power to procure colorful and myriad material circumstance to gratify the gross impulses of a bestial eroticism. The basic seamy side of sexuality is that it is steered by an unenlighted consciousness. Thus, the most dangerous and loathsome thing is when our relatively evolved consciousness demeans itself and panders to gross and unwholesome caprices, which are a creation of the intellect and phantasm and not the sexual drive. Through these, however, the sexual drive expands itself from being blunt and intuitive to being creative, myriad, and experimental of course in the derogatory and material sense. Sexuality thus becomes imbalanced, because it will comprise things not indigenous to its nature and purpose.

Finally, to denote amusingly, both the female and male sexual organs have "an excess of dispensable tissue" the loss of which is the backbone of hefty social/religious rituals, about which we are variably adamant and obsessed: defloration and circumcision.

Historically, sex has been ambivalently the trenchant obsession as well as the effigy of humanity. Sexuality is a formidable factor and touchstone of this world.

The Army

The role and nature of the army is less subject to controversy and criticism, whereas all the other components of the Establishment have been questioned and berated with disparate degrees of revulsion.

Why are there armies?

The heuristic concepts belaying the existence of armies are that the world is not a peaceful place and that warfare is always imminent to be waged. Armies exist with an elementary twofold mission to defend or to offend. Thus, the ambiance that armies create is the threat of defensive or offensive transgressions and violence. This is the seemingly sadistic element. The

masochist element is that soldiers sound to be the
sacrificial lambs of world politics since warfare is
always undertaken fundamentally to satiate economic
ambitions and to protect the hierarchy of political
power and dominion.

In a world politics of global enmity and contest, the
armies are obedient to authority and crystallize the
dehumanizing elements of systematic hierarchy. A
soldier serves his or her country, to the extent to be
willing to kill or be killed for such notions as
patriotism and complete subservience and
capitulation to the mentality and dictations of the
military institution, which is in turn governed by
politics and the "phantoms" that steer global politics.
Hence, the soldier is a socially and militarily
conditioned person, best internalizing the blunt
dogma and political purposes of both, but with a
sense of duty and of valor.

Soldiers can be defined as either militants with a
creedological or mercenary cause. The creed- patterns
of thought, values, and mentality- may range from
patriotism to religious causes.

The absence of world peace throughout history is to
be imputed to politics and to society. The warfare and
international violence forms a continuum with

personal predilections of aggression and interpersonal transgressions, as well as with personal ignorance that collectively engenders our politics. The lamest thing to be said is that war can contribute to the happiness and wellbeing of a human. In an ideal world, armies don't exist, because they are the backbone of a political system.

Soldiers are renowned for their emotional detachment in the way they objectify themselves and others to serve a system. The system is unquestionable as God himself and herself. However, the system is an unjust and unwholesome hierarchy of authority in consonance with a certain dogma or mentality. We are all soldiers of society in this sense to varying extents. Social morality actually sanctions violence and killing, and soldiers for this sake objectify other people that their killing, mutilation, or torture would be assimilated as a necessary act of duty, protection, and dignity. The mostly justified act of violence is self-defense, the thing that doesn't change its essence.

There are many horrific things associated with warfare and thus with soldiers: epic rapes, mutilations, torture, carnage, destruction, slaughters… These are inherent part of our Selves, of our heritage and culture, and of our spiritual capacity.

* A Vision *

If we were so different from these, we wouldn't have been born into this world to face it.

Money

Money is the pillar and marrow of this system.
Without the multifarious significations (social,
economic, political, and spiritual) of money, there
would be no system. It's a unifying factor to all the
diverse aspects of our life bound by a certain
historical mentality.

Money is the most elemental sustenance on which our
lives thrive. Everything from taking a "free" stroll on
the streets, establishing a business, envisaging future
prospects, getting married, answering a social call, to
defining politics is based on money. Money is the
God of this material world, literally omnipresent and
omnipotent.

* A Vision *

A human's work is supposed to be a human's contributions to the welfare and satiation of society, achieved by solidarity and cooperation. It's a great spiritual activity if it were not for money, for money downgrades considerably if not kills the immediacy of the spiritual significations and pleasures of work. Money undermines a potentially great spiritual activity via the enterprise and machinations of a material mentality.

The basic spiritual issue of money as with any aspect of this system is the fact that it objectifies, dehumanizes, and commodifies, people, work, products, and natural resources, as tackled efficiently but fruitlessly by the communists. The issue of the latter is that they have failed in their efforts and aspirations for an endless list of righteous reasons, first and foremost of which is that they have abstained from approaching a human as a spiritual being. They in fact have dehumanized a human through their bland and colorless vision of economic and social equality, if not to say in practice despotic and hypocritical hierarchy: a human was conceived still as a mechanical, callous cog within a system. There was still no consideration to the emotional well-being and spiritual quality of life. With communists, the spirit of material existence and

inclemently political orientation was still pervading
and even more bluntly.

The economic ethics of this system is that of property
and unequal distribution of wealth, vitally necessary
for establishing and maintaining a hierarchy of
authority. The latter insinuates tacitly mass and
historical exploitation of peoples from slavery,
serfdom, aristocracy, commercialism, to sexism
(economic marginalization of women)... In a material
world, property means political power. The latter
means perennial, volatile bloodbath and strife for the
first. In spiritual actuality, property is a dark illusion
at most times and to all humanity, a nightmare better
to be ended.

In consonance with what has been propounded,
money after all is but the manifestation of a certain
spiritual potential and signification indigenous to our
spiritual capacity.

What will happen if we obliterate money?

When the day comes, whence money and this whole
system of the politically purposeful unequal
distribution of wealth will be extirpated, then,
humans will have to work for their souls and for the
communal spirit of a supposedly highly cooperative,

consolidated, and egalitarian society. The welfare of every individual of the global human society will be the ultimate priority, and not the upperhand authority and power as now. There will be no property, no fees, no duality of excessive affluence and needy indignity, and no gory political unrest for power. Property will be communal and the prestigious hierarchy of authority will be forgone and outmoded. The mentality relating to remuneration will be different since a person will feel economically and socially secure and satiated. People will then be truly equal and spiritual. Their work, aspirations, entities, and production wouldn't be reduced and denominated with everything else into a monetary value. All will be more immediately eligible to whatever our human economy, technology, and creativity will burgeon. Above all, the self-contradictory and self-conflicting spirit of human greed, ignorance, exploitation, insecurity, mistrust, wariness, sloth, and gaudy privileges (emotional values underlying the extant economic system) will be transformed into wholesome emotional and mental attitudes.

Because people are not spiritually ready, if we were now to obliterate money and consequently this whole social/economic/political system based on it, there would be utter chaos and riot, since money has become an inherent part of us and our ethos. It's our guiding light, without it how would we be able to confer meaning to our work and life? How would be able to channel the emotions of vanity and pride through the fancy staples as marketed by the media? How would we be able to organize our different affairs by other means? How would we be economically secure? We sure do refuse to forfeit our rightfully earned wealth, after a tedious life of toil and moil, to be socially and economically equal with some moocher. This wouldn't be fair by any standard. A total eradication of money suddenly of course is out of question, because our instinct is somehow steered by and attracted to it. A surrogate plan is to a certain extent what has been promulgated by socialists and communists. To provide a social/economic/political regime in which governments regard their peoples as their children and furnish them equally and progressively with what is needed and contemporary is still very much a far-reached concept in politics, let alone the obliteration of money and property.

This universal system of trade and economics reflects social attitudes and dogma, and the creation of the concept and socioeconomic/political enterprise of money has sprouted from society's "needs", prospects, and mentality. Was it basically the need of human

greed, or simply the righteous exigency to feel
economically secure and one's work acknowledged in
concrete, universal, and unquestionable values? No
matter how far such rhetorical questions will carry us,
money basically reflects and embodies negativity, an
indigenous and necessary one. The obliteration of
money and property is still an idealistic vision, even
not as concrete as hope.

So, money confers a potent value on things, the charm
of increasing digits next to a trusted monetary unit is
unmatched in actual, palpable efficiency. Money
permeates and affects inexorably every aspect of our
Selves and our lives. However, our world and
collective policies, consciousness, and perspectives
revolving about money have self-evidently failed in
achieving a global bliss, synergy, and oneness, since
happiness, higher spirituality, and social welfare,
justice, andequality have never been its purpose,
intention, or action.

Politics

All aspects of the Establishment exist in an interdependent continuum. Our psyches harbor certain predilections and states of mind and being embodying a certain spiritual capacity which then finds expression collectively in society, social morality, and the social ethos. These in turn burgeon and sanction behavior, mentality, mores, and institutions to serve a political purpose. All through out, economics, society, and politics are intertwined. The hierarchy of authority in society, the social ethos, and the social morality are what crystallize in world politics. Hence, the quality of our politics sprouts from our social experience and our spiritual level of consciousness. Ultimately, politics and authority vary with economic power. Thus, if we have maintained that society is the source and field of action of this whole system and its institutions, politics is then where everything's significations wind up, and eventually gets steered. Every system is blunt and somehow self-conscious of its own demise and imminent outmoding and metamorphosing. Ironically, every political system resists change, striving fruitlessly and vehemently to perpetuate itself. Change is hostile to a political mentality. All in all, all political upheavals have yet been superficial and not tackling the spiritual issues of humanity.

We live in a political world, and not a spiritual one. Even religion incites a material approach to our Selves via emphasizing rituals and dogma which belong to the material, relative, and transient aspects of life, in contrast with the Absolute and Transcendental. A backward collective spirit and narrow mentality is what the religious institutions thrive on.

Every minutia of our lives carries a political message and externalizes political values and purposes. A bride is walked down the aisle ideally with her father, who is the Godfather and aboriginally the head of authority and breadwinner in the family. Language is sexist reflecting a historical, formidable sexism in society, and hence political. The change of a woman's surname indicates a change in patriarchal patronage and chaperonage. The rich minority versus the penurious majority is a confounding and overwhelming political issue. Sexuality reflects political attitudes towards sex, gender, and gender roles. Even pornography communicates a political purpose... Basically, the fact that we are living in a political world makes everything that we propound and enact, every way we interact, what and how we think, and everything that the institutions of society elicit laden with political purposes and attitudes, that almost always reinforce our bondage to this system. If we are bound to and by our system-which we are, then our vision and aspirations towards a Unitarian and better humanity will be mitigated, if they were not inexistent all together. Our Establishment has given us our heritage and our history. If we don't deny it, then we must change it.

Politics is ficklish, volatile, and brutal. It has been evolving and flipping between political regimes, in harmony and simultaneity with social and economic changes. Politicians are in the overwhelming majority, feelingless and heartless people. They dehumanize and sacrifice their obedient subjects to serve themselves or some lame political cause. The ultimate political cause is that which creates salvation, which is not inherent and discordant with the nature

and purpose of politics, and it's but a peaceful
collective spiritual quest and fulfillment.

I have finally resolved in commiserating myself that it
has been the best we can do, the best system we can
enact, embody, and experience, within our spiritual
capacity and limitations.

Section Three

Wisdom

All the higher spiritual values and states of being exist in a continuum just as the gross and the ignorant manifest and propagate the same essence and effect in the different facets of our being and lives. Wisdom engenders happiness. Happiness engenders health. A wise person seeks professional and material success so as to elicit wellbeing and progression on all levels, since economic security bolsters the emotional one… So, just as corruption and ignorance are contagious and all-pervading, the same applies to wisdom and the more evolved states of spirituality. The values belonging to each level of consciousness exist in a oneness and in a subtle synergy of interdependence.

Our lack of wisdom has been externalized in our human heritage. I have portrayed the Establishment self-evidently as something hideous, and corroborated that with as many abstract and tangible facts I could muster. So, in other words, our humanity has lacked a state of happiness, welfare, peace, love, and wisdom, first and foremost due to the limitations of our spiritual capacity. Our history, heritage, and experience may be synonymous with infamy and spiritual ignorance, but on some level, this had been a part of God's plan, of the duality of creation. Some higher consciousness witnessing and transcending our experience can't perceive "us" but as good, as an essential part of the balance of the whole creation.

Wisdom and happiness are like a nostalgia, we unawares conceive that we are somewhere not conducive and inclemently oblivious to them. We become what we hate in this world. We are not strong and "equipped" enough to contend and vie with the irresistible flow of our lives, and consequently cave in to the mediocrity. Somehow, all facets of our lives, even our personal convictions and mentality are mechanical, conditioned, stagnant, and unwise. Indeed, life, in its hectic effervescence, overwhelms us, if not to speak of the trials, traumas, hardship, and stress. Then, we discover after a great personal toll of time, errors, and efforts that happiness is a state of emotional health independent of all material variables but ironically also conducive to success and welfare on the material level, that only the wise are truly happy. Their happiness is something that can't be taken away from them if circumstances weather and change.

It sounds that we have been always looking for salvation of our Selves in all the wrong places. We recourse to the material world or to some dimension of our physical experience, and the outcome is either a volatile and friable sense of happiness or a bondage and a plain failure. The first and final recourse and haven to a person is his or her Self.

Physical experience is not without knowledge and a sense of self-fulfillment. If a person is wise, his or her physical and material experience would be by nature with the minimum of negative reverberations. Higher spirituality doesn't mean renouncing the vital and indigenous aspects and activities of our material existence, but it means modulating and amending them to the utmost possible balance, goodness, and health. Even though by necessity all material phenomena are inherently imperfect, the true, indomitable happiness can still thrive if the material experiences are balanced. However, balancing the material experiences is possible but extremely tenuous.

Every physical act or material situation insinuates and externalizes a state of being or an experience of consciousness: a certain relationship of one's ego to one's soul and to God, and a certain karma.

So, wisdom is about spiritual knowledge and its embodiment on all levels and activities of our consciousness, physical activities are the externalization of mental and psychological activities and essences. I have already mentioned that spiritual progression is a continual quest in the sense that it always expands in parallel with the expansion of the universe. In the condition of spiritual enlightenment, a human consciousness reconciles and transcends the fact of the material different and dissonant forms: the discrete physical existence of a human and that of the universe in its different manifestations become one. The myriad material forms are but one on a subtle and sublime level of consciousness and existence. Only an enlighted consciousness can actually "perceive" that with a phenomenal immediacy, I am now only conceiving it in apprehensive contemplation.

I have also mentioned before that wisdom belongs to the Mind of 100% intelligence. We are only inspired and endowed with it, as well as with any grace, since we can't create, we only propound manifestations of spiritual essences. We entertain creativity and not creation. We discover natural laws. Then, we implement these to concoct "creatively" endless inventions.

Stress undermines and mutilates the nature of the human consciousness. It's extant when the consciousness gets overwhelmed in its material existence. Every physical or psychological experience relays and metamorphoses karma and stress, by either propounding further negativity or further happiness. Negativity overwhelms the consciousness since it has the spiritual potential of prolonging the extent of material experience, shifting the dimensions of relativity by the law of karma and thus depleting a person's spiritual and physical stamina and wellbeing. Any emphasis on the material aspects almost always transgresses the balanced. It's like choosing to wallow in the "myriad of forms" represents the illusively bitter-sweet karma- the protracted way to enlightenment- antithetical to the oneness and spiritual immediacy of the balanced material experiences. So, naturally, if karma emphasizes the material experiences of a person, it will be inclusive of a myriad of imbalanced experiences in the purpose to exhaust them in order to arrive at a full-fledged knowledge. A person would then be drenched and enervated by the frenzy and furor of his or her outward experience, and left with little or no potential to recourse to the peaceful haven of the Self. Then, happiness will be a meager and pending state.

The consciousness intuitively is endowed with the spiritual capacity to heal itself with variable degrees of immediacy. If we are expanding our awareness concerning our karma, experience, and Selves, then our way to wisdom, health, and happiness will be most immediate. On the other hand, if we wallow in any form of negativity, we'll be propounding more karma and more experience, procrastinating and extending our quest of inner serenity, self-knowledge, and finally enlightenment.

Prayer is the initiative of the phenomenon of recuperation and redemption from ignorance and the negative states of being. Christ has said that prayer shouldn't be something mechanical, ritualistic, forced, and emotionally vapid, as the religious institution propagandizes. A prayer is something very personal and very subjective. It's the attempt of the human relative consciousness to communicate with the

Highest Absolute Consciousness. Hence, prayer is the communion and the haven we resort to in striving to embody better states of consciousness and being.

Prayer is an intimate activity of self-knowledge and self-realization: knowing what are our spiritual shortcomings and aberrations (increased awareness), then soliciting divine and transcendental help to forgive, redeem, and amend our consciousness, and finally gratefully enjoying the triumph and wonder of spiritual revelation and deliverance from ignorance. Spiritual ignorance makes us embody negative states of mind and being.

Wisdom transcends mere intelligence. Intelligence translates itself objectively whereas wisdom translates itself both subjectively and objectively. A genius may not be wise. An illiterate may be the wisest of men. If the intellect forgoes wisdom, it most immediately and innately castrates its potential and creates great karma on itself. The intellect may propound great negativity, and all negative experiences and states of mind and being are inherently with limited, castrated, and downgraded physical and spiritual potentials. For instance, science may pride itself with its weapons of mass destruction, ironically, these are the self-same instruments to elicit the backwardness of our humanity on all levels, from humanitarian to material considerations, since weapons by the virtue of the political game and the ill-intentions underpinning them can also kill those who concocted them. Furthermore, this scientific mentality is oblivious to the karma it begets to itself.

All higher states of consciousness propagate and are charged with more energy. If a person becomes wrathful, his energy level would be depleted, which takes its toll on his physical potentials and personal wellbeing most directly. Each state of being requires the same energy it propounds. It takes more energy to make you happy than to make you sad. Also, being happy makes one more vivacious and vibrant. Thus, each state of being propounds and embodies the self-same amount of energy. At this point, it's a matter of will.

Wisdom is the quest for spiritual knowledge and happiness. It purgates one's being from the impurities and negativity that clogs and hinders one's consciousness and one's spiritual progression, which is also intertwined with wellbeing on the physical level. A hermit renounces almost all material aspects: it's his or her formula of adjusting his or her Self to the world while he or she pursues wisdom. While we householders can't do that, our wellbeing thrives on how we pursue both the quest for material welfare and security and the quest for spiritual progression. Spirituality is not hostile to materialism, as long as materialism comprises the balanced aspects of material existence, which embody wisdom.

Pleasures

Are there many kinds and sorts of pleasure? Or is the perception of pleasure relative with respect to all the different pleasurable situations conducive to the same exact kind and nature of pleasure in different degrees of intensity? Is pleasure tax-free? Can pleasure be a conception, a perennial state of being, in stead of being a limited, relative-to material conditions, and unduly brief perception?

The pursuit of pleasure is the most natural of urges having the innate need to satisfaction, communion, and happiness its launching point. From there, the pursuit of pleasure may trespass the natural and balanced forms into the realms of unnaturality: it gets deformed by a stressed consciousness engendering more of the stressful state of mind that elicited it. Pleasures are different, versatile, and relative to a number of variable issues: state of mind, level of consciousness, karma, physical and spiritual balance, retribution... Different kinds of pleasure embody different levels of consciousness and spirituality. Furthermore, pleasures are stimulated by different material and physical conditions: it's how much these are balanced and wholesome, and what spirituality they embody, that demarcates whether the pleasure is entwined with a retribution of misery to be unraveled by the effect of time and karma.

There's something about our consciousness that at countless times perceives poignantly our existence as extremely and minatorily excruciating and insufferable. Then, it would be high-time for us to numb our consciousness and resort to pleasure: usually alcohol, drugs, promiscuity, greed, and authority. This is the vicarious choice of pursuing wisdom and happiness, what we truly lack. However, it's bondage to the mediocre materialism of our world that induces us to forfeit our individual spiritual progression, and further ensnares us in the destructive continuum of spiritual ignorance, flopping between gross pleasures and their ensuing retributions of disease, misery, isolation, restlessness, violence, and negativity.

Happiness is the utmost continual and extensive state of pleasure. As it matures in one's being, it evolves to less illusiveness and to less of the painful sense of transience, always seeking more of itself. Happiness and wisdom are intertwined and exist on the same plane of being. Because our happiness is dynamic and expands, it forces our consciousness to expand with it. It sheds light on darkness, making us momentarily feel guilty and incredulous. Thus, happiness creates pain, but the pain it creates is most immediate to spiritual revelation and further deliverance from ignorance and stress. It's of utmost mildness. The quest for happiness is the self-same quest for wisdom. The truest sense of happiness is achieved by freedom, the emancipation from one's relativity of consciousness and experience, by a state of physical existence that utmost approaches the nil: in food, sex, physical contact... That's an ideal, and our reality is very much discrepant. However, as stated before, the balanced material formulas of existence embody oneness literally. That is, for instance, monogamy embodies oneness versus all the countless plethora of the imbalanced possibilities: promiscuity of the man, promiscuity of the woman, of both, the extent of the promiscuity, the imbalance of the sexual acts, homosexuality... These are the "myriad of forms", which eventually one day will balance themselves into material inexistence, affiliated of course with the subtle transformation of energies. Tacitly, happiness is exclusively relative to the balanced material aspects. All material phenomena are inherently unstable and imperfect, even the balanced. That's why they are ever-changing and transforming, exhausting themselves. The same applies to happiness which is a state of being since happiness is created in duality with sadness, thus they are not transcendental aspects.

Eroticism is the grosser form of pleasure created by unwholesome physical situations, by the licentious pursuit of the material specious pleasures. Eroticism may be induced anywhere from drugs, sexually imbalanced acts, to social actions of ill-intent... It is when we project and attach to material experiences the happiness we do not feel about them, that can't be engendered by them, for it's not inherent to their imbalanced nature. Eroticism is the vain, empty pleasure. Thus, eroticism is the emotional quality that enhances illusively our bondage to the gross and begets relatively massive karma. Eroticism is the negative side of pleasure, either one is oriented towards happiness or eroticism, using religious terminology, towards heaven or hell.

Pleasures are relative to our consciousness as manifest through our mentality: our values, prejudices, imperfections, self-righteousness, knowledge, intentions... Through our mentality, we unconsciously seek the pleasure that is relatively "meaningful", that our psyche sanctions and justifies for us, and that satiates our urge for self-fulfillment. All in all, pleasures are either gross or balanced.

Emotional Void

Emotional void souses us in desperation and anxiety, pushing us to seek unwise diversions, usually in extreme material experiences, which have trespassed the skirts of the balanced. The choice of pursuing "meaningful pleasures" in the material aspects without spiritual considerations, makes pleasure a mechanical addiction and a monotonous ritual which by necessity will elicit the transgression of the relatively balanced and healthy experiences to the extreme and imbalanced. The imbalanced and the "dark" come with a bondage. Bondage to some sorts of pleasure and experiences embodying spiritual ignorance comes with a terrible retribution, starting with the immediate state of mind and well-being to the self-same reverberations on oneself of the vibrations which one has propounded: the retribution commensurate to the state of consciousness, but altering the relativity. If one has expended time and effort in entertaining negativity, whether by thought, intention, or deed, one will further experience karma and protract his or her way to spiritual knowledge in misallocating his or her potentials.

Each person should create a world of his or her own, a world of an emotional safety net, a world of spirituality to recourse to or at exigencies to rebound on: first and foremost, a personal repertoire of wisdom and faith, a realization that one at times will be alone, solitary, and headlong encountering the trials of consciousness, that externalize in different material circumstances and hardships. One by his or her emotional safety net will confer meaning, security, and hope to his or her existence, and will further enjoy material and manifest blessings with a sense of ease and security. All material experiences whether joyful or painful are transient, but all experiences lead to wisdom, whether by the long or short way relative to what karma one creates. Converging one's emotional furor inwardly is the key to health, since after all every material manifestation that is so crucial and meaningful to a person is a state imputed to his or her own innate predilections and needs. In other words, because you are what you are attracts and attaches you to a certain aspect.

Emotional void translates into an interplay between restlessness and stagnation, an unrest and a disquietude. All negativity in its different forms of disease, misery, ignorance, affliction, emotional void… is the incarnation of the retribution to one's lack of wisdom. We must be tried by God for we lack wisdom, but trials can be attenuated and undergone with the minimum spiritual loss and personal casualties, by reducing our perception of "stress". So, emotional affliction is the pungent taste of God's trials, making the latter most meaningful and most real, anything that is real is which makes the consciousness "intuitively aware" of its meaning and nature via the involved reaction of the emotional agency. This is what belays the demarcation between objective and subjective knowledge, the latter has the great potential to evolve and transcend since it's emotionally meaningful and thus truthful. Objective knowledge is relatively hypocritical.

Alas, at times, life becomes so unduly insufferable that we pusillanimously scuttle into bitter, pernicious pleasures to vent up our disappointment and frustration, the eroticism of material imbalances.

A person in a relative state of happiness is like an unperturbed lake which is so immaculate that it reflects the blueness of the sky and the viridity of nature around. All is sensuously beautiful. However, because we lack wisdom, trials must be underwent to put us through excruciating pain and deliver us afterwards, usually with a sense of greater insight and maturity. Consequently, some people -represent humanity and the world it has created- passing by the lake are so adamant to stir the clear waters. If the waters are shallow, the lake will get torpid and perturbed. Metaphorically, this happens to a person's experience with the world when he or she lacks wisdom. In times of serenity, one should garner wisdom for times of trial which can be radically attenuated. On the other hand, as the waters get deeper, it will be harder to perturb the serenity of the lake. The most ideal stance is when the lake is deep and when the soil and sediments in its bottom allow for a minimum of torpidity. The sediments represent a person's karma, the waste and impurities one necessarily creates and will one day need to be managed.

Sufficely, an emotional void is due to a breach or deficit in one's rapport with oneself and in one's communion with God, a matter that should be resolved in this inward realm. The desperation, vapidity, and ennui are but a syndrome. Our classical behavior is to resort vicariously to the gross aspects of materialism to numb our aching consciousness, which is tacitly entwined with a pernicious retribution.

Love

Love is a continual prayer for the expansion of goodness, peace, and beauty. Basically, love is an attitude-antithetical to all negative essences- towards oneself, God, and the rest of creation. All wisdom and happiness evolve about this emotional quality in its relation to life, the massive reclamatory effect of this intuitive, elementary force. To denote, all emotional qualities are the essence of mental attitudes, since all dogma, values, and patterns of thought engender a certain state of being. Your emotional qualities define what vibrations you propound in life and what intentions you hold towards the issues of your spiritual and personal progression, and by implication what contributions you are making to the embodiment and propagation of bliss outwardly and

inwardly, in all its higher spiritual values like
solidarity, generosity, trust, truth, justice, mercy,
welfare, health,...

Negative emotions from hatred to anger are self-
righteously and egocentrically justified. Egocentricity
is often considered to be the selfish and
indiscriminate pursuit of one's detached good and
profligate pleasure. Well, I believe that egocentricity
is an illusion and an ignorance, an eroticized pleasure
coming with a terrible retribution that hinders one's
progression and wellbeing. Eroticism embodies
spiritual ignorance and hence begets karma to
equipoise what has been propounded. It is the
essence of egocentricity, the emotional quality of
bondage. When the pleasure is not indigenous to a
certain aspect or experience in life (namely, the
balanced and the healthy aspects of materialism), and
hence not perceived intuitively, the pleasure is the
then perfunctory and eroticized, egocentrically
processed and projected. Egocentricity is the mental
attitude that presumes and feigns the truth. The
virtue of egocentricity is that it provides plausible,
reasonable justification for all the misery, anger,
promiscuity, violence, hatred, condemnation, and all
the other forms of spiritual ignorance. The repertoire
of egocentricity is directly proportional to the

potential of the objective intelligence. Thus, egocentricity is proud ignorance.

Love reconciles and reclaims all, the inwardly and outwardly oriented states of being and attitudes. Love makes enemies friends. Love engenders serenity inside and peace with all others and with life. Love is forgiveness, generosity, and harmony. It is insight, humility, and self-knowledge, a form of divine inspiration that just needs from you your attention and good will. All in all, love, this ever-expanding happy communion, is wisdom heartfelt and embodied on an intimate and truthful level, eradicating all negative attitudes towards any issue, experience, or person. One of the best examples of humanity's embodiment of the spirit of love is sainthood. Saints or hermits are generous in bestowing their blessings on others. They don't condemn a person even if he or she reeks with sin. They know it's not their job. They seek only to propagate the spirit of love and happiness.

This book has upheld monogamy as the ideal formula whence one's sexual and emotional drives are unified and reconciled in one person: one's soul-mate. All the multitude of relationships will eventually wind up to one person. Hence, they were illusions of communion and of the wholeness engendered by love. They were pastimes to condole our loneliness, isolation, egocentricity, and spiritual ignorance. They were the momentary, brief pleasure that would vaporize into thin air, leaving behind them an emotional void and bolstering the terrible sense of disappointment and chagrin. So, we'll then be in need to seek more and more bittersweet or rather bitter pastimes in reaction to our emotional void. It's this self-same emotional emptiness which has incited us in a mood of anxiety, desperation, and anger to resort to spiritually unwholesome acts. From there, all was a perfunctory, insipid, repetitive cycle, with a need each time to augment the degree and dosage of the gross prescription and vary its forms. It was an addiction, a bondage to either loveless relationships (which embodies an emotional quality of emptiness) or relationships were love is inadequately misplaced and distorted, that inevitably propagated its unhappy, unwise essence to other facets of our life and experience. Then, we meet our soul-mate, we feel the wonder of a spiritual revelation, and spiritual purgation ensues in various degrees and towards different levels of consciousness to various people. Thus, a person's truest and most viable emotional communion is with one's soul-mate.

Love has a miraculous transformatory power. It inspires goodness and wisdom, impervious to all the unholy and unwholesome acts perpetrated in its name. Love is the impetus of life, endowing it with happiness and hence making it emotionally meaningful and beautiful in the utmost fundamental way. Love is communion: with God, wisdom, one's soul-mate, nature, other people...

I have so far been non-artistic, but now I have the intention to entertain you, to toy around with my vision. So, help me God.

Phoebus

There are many lonely men and women in this world, all eager to fall in love someday and hopefully not out of it: to feel whole and emotionally secure with someone. It's a universal classical formula, with always a vitally pungent taste.

Phoebus, the shepherd, was grazing his livestock somewhere near Athens in the year 525 B.C. He was watching over his sheep and Athena and Aphrodite were watching over him, actually having a fiery conversation. His sighting has spurred an ancient, unsettled debate between them about love, whether love is physical or spiritual, whether a creature's innate nature prefers a plethora of sexual partners or one. Does love beget misery

or happiness? Is love a freedom or a prison? Which form of
love is the best choice...?

Aphrodite: (scornfully) dear my sister, do you really
believe what you are saying? That one partner can
bring more happiness than many. Oh, my poor waif. I
never thought you were this naïve! Why have one if
you can have and enjoy many. You should give an
edge to your existence. Indulge your body. Go to
extremes and beyond them. Trespass limits. There's
no limit...
Athena: there's death you see...
Aphrodite: oh please... Leave death out of it... We
don't die.
Athena: no, I meant that death is one of the limits.
There's disease...
Aphrodite: oh, I see... you mean spiritual death...
pretty wise... Since we are discussing love matters
and you are bringing in mere abstractions to justify
how lame and boring you live in reality, I own that
you are right. Disease is a limit. Diseased men and
women can't make love vigorously and are not
efficient partners. I am not talking about them. They
are not a part of life, they are a part of death.
Athena: disease is a trial and a retribution.
Aphrodite: sister I can't believe with all your wisdom
how at times truly heartless you are! Where is your
pity...!

Athena: both trial and retribution come from the
dearth of wisdom.
Aphrodite: (mimicking) lack of wisdom...preacher
you. So, you are saying if life sees people lacking
something, it causes them pain for their deficiency,
sprinkling salt on the wound...
Athena: this sexuality you are talking about is about
the lack of wisdom...
Aphrodite: so it's wrong to enjoy one's physical
existence. If sex is too bad, why life created us with
sexual organs, expecting us to err and then to punish
us mercilessly for our brief happiness... Life sounds
begrudging, arbitrary, and despotic...do you expect
me to believe that this is the essence of life, this
wisdom of yours... (laughing hysterically) hey
sister...congratulate yourself for you have made me
serious for a second... who needs wisdom when you
got pleasure...
Athena: pleasure doesn't last long and you know it.
That is why you keep seeking more of it. It gives you
emptiness and restless anticipation.
Aphrodite: you are mistaken. That's just a part of it.
You forgot to mention how pleasure tastes. Why
people are willing to suffer for it. You should
experience things more.
Athena: I am sister. I experience things in my mind to
know and understand them. But I don't want to
become all the things I know.

Aphrodite: we become the things we hate.
Athena: I know no hate and I am not
condemning...hate creates emotional bondage to the
object of hatred. Any emotional frenziful obsession
can turn to its direct opposite if given just the right
stimulus. We have the innate, indelible drive to
reconcile ourselves to life, and at certain extreme
situations we unconsciously and abruptly become
what we hate.
Aphrodite: you do impress me Athena. (silence)
You do impress me Athena, for a virgin, you are truly
sensuous...
Athena: I am not a virgin. I am wed to my lover.
Aphrodite: nonsense. You had none...never dared...
Athena: he's not physically present yet...
Aphrodite: (baffled and dispirited) I can't but own
it... your secret perplexes me with utmost greatness,
for I am not wise, sister...
Athena: I have none...
Aphrodite: what?
Athena: secrets...
Aphrodite: I've had many lovers who thought they
had withheld secrets from me...I know what secrets
are. They are matters incapable of being seen or
understood...
Athena: it depends...
Aphrodite: on what?
Athena: on you...

Aphrodite: (on her knees, holding Athena and beseeching her) oh, my dear sister Athena… I've always wanted to tell you this. It has been so distressing to me. I can't but confess to you. I have ruined all my lovers, and they are plentiful… some of them have truly believed themselves to be totally in love. I not only hurt them I destroyed them utterly, driven them to suicide and death…most of the times, I'd love somebody to enjoy my body with him in a physical union, our passionate lustful bodies striving to get connected and involved and then delivered from a strange mixture of pleasure and pain. It's like dying and getting re-born. But after our love-making, my love for him would get treacherous and rove somewhere else.

Athena: it was only desire…

Aphrodite: if he was a good, virile lover, he'll be able to buy himself a couple of more times with the Goddess…but all in all, my love for him will either dwindle considerably or vanish. And his love for me will get stronger, for I am a goddess and he's just a man. As you say, it must be something about the fatal bondage to natural forces beyond one's capacity to cope with successfully, which I think now that I embody… (desperately) oh, Athena help me for I admit I am incapable of love. I admit to only know intense physical desire and pleasure, by which I bring

intense psychological torture and terrible retribution
on those men…
*Seeing Athena so stiff and unaffected and growing more
mindful to impress her.*
…the retribution for straying, taking me as a lover,
denying their souls and the women who were truly
meant for them… it's a game they couldn't master…
Athena: (dryly) what you want?
Aphrodite: I want the secret of love, true love…
Athena: (outraged but peaceful) you are evil just as
your soul-mate… you have denied eachother by your
debauchery, unnaturality, the havoc you wreaked on
others. your ignorance…
Aphrodite: well, enlighten me who is my soul-mate.
Athena: never mind...
Aphrodite: then cure me. Be my salvation. Give me
the secret of love. Doesn't love have high healing
powers…?
Athena: life can only unravel this secret to you. Life
can decide if you are ready and eligible or not… I am
totally aware my sister that this is not but another of
your wiles.
Aphrodite: we'll see about that.
*Suddenly, Aries appears, and holds Athena firmly from
behind threatening to slit her throat with his sling.*
Athena: so, you have been planning this for a while.
Aphrodite gloats disdainfully.
Athena: it will not work.

Aphrodite: you'll see…

Athena: I prefer to die…then, Zeus will…

Aries: (interruptingly) well, we don't really care.

Athena: (uneasy) oh, yes you do…let's make a deal. (struggling) let go… I'll give you love's secret to use and abuse as much as you chose if that shepherd over there chooses to have it too…

Aphrodite: what? Are you joking? Of course he will…

Athena: on one account. That we leave him rationalize and not meddle whatsoever for one hour.

And so the two Goddesses orbed to Phoebus and lured him with this great offer.

Phoebus: oh, don't go wait. I accept. I accept. Oh, this doesn't need any thinking, it's so beautiful. Imagine the great power I'll have over women. I'll love them and they'll love me fully. Though I can't make love to them all at the same time. But then, love mostly is spiritual. So, we, me and my women, we'll be always in a spiritual communion together though not physical…but then…

Enters Lydia. Runs to him.

Lydia: (hugging him) oh, Phoebus…I so missed you. We have always been together from the time of our childhood and then you disappear suddenly for a whole week. You can't believe how long it was. Are you doing well? I've been searching all over for you….

Phoebus: oh, Lydia my dear dear friend...I can't believe that you are the first person to know...
Lydia: know what?
Phoebus: you will not believe this. Aphrodite and Athena made this most amazing apparition on me and offered to endow me with the secret of love...
Lydia: (tentatively and uncertain) do you have it now?
Phoebus: oh no, they stipulated that I should deliberate for an hour freely...not under their watch.
Lydia: and how are you doing?
Phoebus: well yes, I am very excited. Just think of the endless potentials of it...
Lydia: potentials? What you mean?
Phoebus: well I was thinking...just think of how many women I'll be able to love and be loved back. Think of the multiplied joy of this multiple communion.
Lydia: (dispirited, unenthusiastic) oh yes...well, goodluck.
Phoebus: (shocked) what? Aren't you happy for me... Don't you want my good?
Lydia: well yes sure. If that's what you want.
Phoebus: (aggressively) yes, it's what I want and what I will enjoy...
Lydia: well, do you want anything else from me. I got to get back home. I slipped out secretly... I'll be missed.

Phoebus: well what you think? Come stay just a little more. Tell me your point of view my dearest dearest friend. Advise me. I hate to see you silent and speechless like this. It kills me.

Lydia: can I be honest?

Phoebus: (perplexed) well yes sure.

Lydia: I believe that true love is only between two people, two soul-mates destined by life and fate to be together and to complete one another…

Phoebus: I'll think about it…

A brooding silence between them…

Lydia: what is your nature?

Phoebus: what you mean?

Lydia: I mean aren't you a human and aren't they goddesses. Do you think you'll be able to handle such an enormous gift and ability with it not firing back at you…?

Phoebus: I never looked at it this way…

With Lydia's pending hopes starting to reblossom, they were rended curtly.

Phoebus: Lydia…please don't be pessimistic and not loving life. Oh, dear Lydia one more important thing. I can't but ask you for I have great feelings for you as you know (seizing and fondling her hands) do you want to be the dearest and most special one of my lovers?

Lydia: (outraged) of course not.

Upon which he fell struck and bereaved as if by a bolt from Zeus.

Phoebus: what?? What are you talking about? We both know about our feelings for eachother…how can you be so rude and insensitive? Why were you offended by my offer? You have been my queen since we were children. And you still are. You'll always be my queen. I'll enjoy spending most of my time with you… you know we have something special…

Lydia: why don't I find that tempting?

Phoebus: (incensed) what?? I can't believe this…maybe…maybe because you don't love me…never did…maybe you found another man to fill my place during last week…best of luck. Go away.

Lydia: (holding her sob) I will go away… forever…because I don't want to be one of your many lovers, I thought you were another man…and yes, I had loved you before now. But right now and at this moment my love for you, well it's you who have ended it… (hurrying away, sobbingly)

Phoebus: (screaming) well, run away but try not to enter Hades by the shortness of your sight…

Lydia gone

(furiously) she doesn't deserve me… she doesn't but oh,…(falling into hysterical crying. Then, whining) oh, please. Come back. Don't go. (getting up to his feet to run after her)

Aphrodite: well where are you going? Stay here the hour is over.

Phoebus: get out of my way. I can't.

Aphrodite: you can't what?

Phoebus: I can't stay here anymore. I must be somewhere else...with someone.

Athena: so you don't want our gift?

Aphrodite: let's not hurry. Please be wise Phoebus.

Phoebus: no. I don't want that gift I don't need it. It's the cause of my misery right now...of our misery...I now see...

Hurrying away after Lydia...

Athena: that's why I am wise Aphrodite. Evermore than you. I wish that you'll be wise someday... That means you're not getting the secret.

Aphrodite: well, what are you talking about...? I've seen the secret of love in a concrete example. (skeptically) Do you think they'll love eachother forever?

Athena: yes. All of Athens will talk of Phoebus' love for Lydia and Lydia's love for Phoebus. They'll be happy and wise and have a beautiful life and family...almost like an idyllic portrait... Phoebus and Lydia are but one physical manifestation of the infinity of potentials for love between two soul-mates entwined together by the hands of the Gods of fate and of life to serve a higher purpose. It's the ultimate blessing that makes all life better...it's but a vehicle for wisdom...

Aphrodite: well, I believe in what I've seen and experienced...I know of love's treachery, infidelity, vanity, cruelty, disrespect, and many other countless evils...

Athena: that is not what love is...

The End

* A Vision *

Regards,
Maysaa Haidar

* A Vision *

www.ingramcontent.com/pod-product-compliance
Lightning Source LLC
Chambersburg PA
CBHW020506100426
42813CB00030B/3137/J